Goshawk, Antelope

Books by Dave Smith

Goshawk, Antelope
Cumberland Station
The Fisherman's Whore
Mean Rufus Throw Down

Limited Editions
In Dark, Sudden with Light
Drunks
Bull Island

Goshawk, Antelope

Poems by Dave Smith

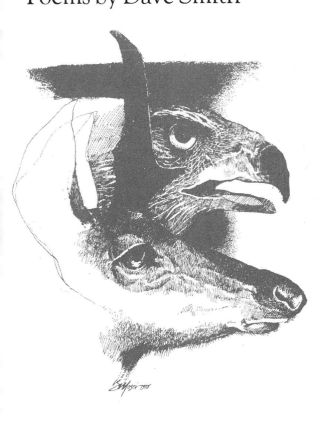

University of Illinois Press
Urbana, Chicago, London

The author wishes to express his thanks to the National
Endowment for the Arts for a Fellowship in Poetry (1976),
which helped him complete this collection.

Drawing by Barry Moser

Library of Congress Cataloging in Publication Data

Smith, David Jeddie, 1942–
  Goshawk, antelope.

  I. Title.
PS3569.M5173G6   811'.5'4   79–14290
ISBN 0–252–00742–5

Many of the poems collected here first appeared in the following publications:

American Poetry Review: "Morning Light: Wanship, Utah" "Hawktree" "Between the Moon and the Sun" "A Moment of Small Pillagers" "Over the Ozarks, Because I Saw Them, Stars Came" "Convulsion" "That Moment, Which You Could Love, What of It"

Ascent: "Hospital Memory During Storm" "Antelope Standing, Some Lying" "To Anyone Hunting Agates on a Pacific Beach" "A Fixation with Birds" "Sea Change: The Rented House at Seal Rock, Oregon" "Corner Room, Hog-Scald in the Air" "Loon" "A Gold of Birds" "Night, Our Hands Parting the Blue Air"

Aura: "Black Widow"

Georgia Review: "Pine Cones"

Hudson Review: "Raw Light, Mountain Lake" "The White Holster" "In the Yard, Late Summer"

Iowa Review: "The Sound of a Silk Dress" "Under the Scrub Oak, a Red Shoe"

Ironwood: "The True Sound of the Goshawk" "A Memory at the Edge of Swollen Rivers"

The Nation: "Chinaberry Tree" "Hath the Drowned Nothing to Dream?"

New Yorker: "Goshawk, Antelope" "Treehouse" "Waving" "August, on the Rented Farm" "Messenger" "The Roundhouse Voices" "The Collector of the Sun" "Rain Forest"

North American Review: "The Dark Eyes of Daughters" (originally "Pickles") "These Promises, These Lost, in Sleep Remain to Us"

Poetry: "Apples in Early October" "Willows, Pond Glitter" "Dreams in Sunlit Rooms"

Porch: "Settlement"

Prairie Schooner: "The Suicide Eater" "On the Limits of Resurrection"

Quarterly West: "Playing Ball"

Three Rivers Poetry Journal: "Dandelions"

Western Humanities Review: "Waking among Horses" "Greenheart Fern" "In Snow, a Possible Life"

For Dee, and for Larry Lieberman,
        always sustainers —

Contents

Now, gently drowsing, she remembers the whistle blowing.
It surrounds space, time, sleepy summer evenings many years
ago: a remote sad wail involving sleep and memory and
somehow love. They'd fight on summer nights because it was
hot and Maudie cried and the icebox made a dripping noise,
and because the whistle blew. But they loved each other,
and the whistle — now it's a part of sleep and darkness, things
that happened long ago: a wild, lost wail, like the voice of
love, passing through the darkened room and softly wailing,
passing out of the sphere of sound itself and hearing.

William Styron
Lie Down in Darkness

Messenger

for John Gardner

MESSENGER

It was not kindness, but I was only buckle-high in the door.
I let him in because the knock had come, the rain
clawed each window and wall. I was afraid.
Climbing down the stairs I did not know
how my country, cunningly, had rotted,
but hear, now, my steps creak in memory
and the rocks let go in the blind nightglass
where you get up, frightened, to reenact
the irrational logic of flesh.

Even now I can't see why it happens, the moment of change,
but must try to witness each particular index
of landscape and irony of promise. I know
I was a child when the banging began, sleepless
with every light in the house blazing. Then
the man whose speech entangled me came in
from the mud-world. He could not
put together the clear words of hope
we dream, only the surge of a river.
He, who said it wasn't a fit thing

for anyone, half-grown, to have to imagine in this godforsaken
life, said there was a message, the river high,
no chance. I remember the wind at that door
breaking like a father's hand on my face.
Such hurting does not cease and maybe
that is why the man went on fumbling
for love, for the loving words
that might be knowledge. He gave me

this message. I took it, and took, without warning, grief's
language that piece-by-piece has showed me how
to connect dreamed moments skidding like rocks
in the silence of a Wyoming midnight.
Each of his rainy words, fragments
of the old sickness, passed into me,
then he was gone, miserable and emptied,
and I had no home but the heart's hut,
the blistering walls of loneliness,
the world's blue skymiles of longing.

Common with drowned fir and uncoiling crocus, then, I
walked in ignorance and entered this terrible life
that was always a dream of the future
in the relentless unsleep of those
who cannot remember the last thing they wanted
to say: that love exists. And in darkness
you have dreamed me into your world
with their message, their words
whispering an hour before black, sudden knocking

that, even as I recall it, begins in your heart's meat
to reverberate, oh, its noise is going
to wake you like a dove's desire.
This is the dream of the soft buckling
of flesh, the beautiful last erosions,
and I swear I would give up these words
if I could, I would stop the code
of that streetlight just beyond your bed—

but it is too late, for the secret of hope swells in you
and who can stop the news that already screams
like the roof's edge leaving its nails
over your child's bed that is, now,
splintered and empty as every moment
skidding at the back of your neck? Leaves
not a month old hurl out of the storm
and steady splatter of time, and tomorrow
will lie still ripening, but only long enough
for you to catalog, in dream, what was possible

before the rake must drag its scritch-scratch over ground.
All I ask is that you turn to the child
inside, those words dreaming and changeless
as love's last chance—let them be said
against whatever, crying in the night,
we still think may be stopped, the black
historical fact of life's event
crashing, like a wall of water,
over the actuary's lawn and yours.

You have seen me before and would not hear, stung by your
wife's fierce beauty, when I called your name,
and the day your mother died I begged
your attention and got your dollar.
I followed you once, in New York, like truth,
always to give you the message, and now
on your porch, mud-spattered, I am
knocking to make you see what love is.
Call your wife, the police, anyone you like,

for everyone is waiting. We don't mean to be unkind but are
compelled to deliver, faithfully, the words
that have been fluttering in your ear
like a scream. It is not the wind
waking you, but the low roar of years
fumbling to tell you what has happened,
or will, when the door flies open
and the naked message of love
stands there stuttering in your face,
alive, crying, leaving nothing out.

RAW LIGHT, MOUNTAIN LAKE

The world has gone swimming in the night
and now, stepping from your bedroom,
you see the dream goes on without you.
As if you were only the quickened musk
of an ancestral trunk momentarily opened,
the dazzled world stands still to remember.
It is as if you were something and are now
almost something, but are not. Motion,
shadow half in memory. The world is full,
you are of this fullness, only you are
what the world cannot remember in first
raw light and nakedness. It waits a moment
like a woman shivering, dark water still
on her, ankle deep in mist, the sun purple
bright in each curve and coiling particular,
raking you with passion. Why have you lived
if not for this love? Only it waits in a cry
of elementals nothing explains, nothing,
and does not seem to understand you.
The world stares at you like a moronic angel.
That is why the rage crawls and the scream,
wordless as a nightwind, pulls the lips back
on your sharp teeth. *Keep me, keep me, keep
me* the bird drills through pines playing
over the water. But this morning
your arm did not fall casually on whatever
you loved, your blood chilled. Now words
fail, or the world does not hear, and now
the slit of your dream fills with dust,
losing the shape you were, becoming
someone walking the path, waving goodbye.

8

GOSHAWK, ANTELOPE

Against snowpeaks, that country of blue sedge and shimmer
of distance rising into his tiny skull full of desire, he
fell across my windshield, a dot at sixty, and I, half-

looking for a place I had never seen, half-dreaming rooms
where blind miles of light lie on framed family faces,

saw him before he was anything, a spot above the glassy road
and in my eye, acetylene burned by brightness and hours
of passage. I saw memory. He came

out of the strange clouded horizon like the dark of whipped
phone wires and the quiet of first feathering shingles
in storm or in the hour of burial,

and dropped into absence where the antelope stood alive
at the fence of barbed wire, horns lifted slightly,
hovering on hooves' edge as if bored with the prospect
of leaps, long standing and still. The wind-

darted dust gave no image beyond itself, puffballs that turned
clockwise and counter-clockwise as he stood
changeless beneath that sudden whistle
of gray. I felt my heart

within those lovely shoulders flame and try to buck off
whatever the air had sent down as shapeless as obsession
and stopped my car, knowing already how
easily the talons dispossessed

all who, without illusions, lived. Dark and light bucked,
clung, shredded in me until I was again a boy on a fence,
hunched near the dream-contending world. But

someone far off was calling and I could not undream
what held me. Though I stood
at last it was late, too late. Someone
called and the legs I had always trusted broke
but not in time and I fell from all chance
to change what was done or undone.

In Wyoming, in June, it was already starcold
though the mild blue of dusk beat back my mother's pain
when I saw him, small as a wind, shriek for the cliffs,
his dream gone, the aching wingless shoulders of the antelope
risen from a low mound of rocks, running from what was
unseen and there, like the red print of a hand

about to fall, for I was late and wishing to God for a tree
to hide under and see for once what had died
out of my life but would never leave or
come back as it had been

like the slow growth of an antelope's legs into freedom
and away from desire's black whirling dream. It was
late, there had been no sign, no reason

to move except the call that might have been only dreamed,
but once I stood under the keening moon that, in Wyoming,
owns all that is and I begged the stars not to come
gouging my bitter and motherless sleep

where I lay long and longed, as I do now over barbed wire,
for the peace of the night-gleaming peaks and the flare
of absence that came, had fallen into

the accusing goshawk face of my father in that dark room
where I walked too late, where the glowing fur-tufts
of candle shadows drift on her face and his

and what was held has become, suddenly, lost like breath.

APPLES IN EARLY OCTOBER

Something has happened: the white meat of the shed-siding
seeps, the snail's foot slickers from his house
lost in a week of red dust. Why is it

the earth gleams like the long-buried crown of a princess?
The stars, the stars stare down diffidently.
A pail by a well pours its emptiness.

Every night now the summons comes and something that
winks red as her first scarf and leaves, when she walks,
no longer hiss, for they are sapless and sodden

as the keening dead under the fieldstone floor of Virginia.
Something has been moving and she has heard it coldly
coiling like the creek, but it is not the creek

waking her from the dream. A gaudy blue flares in her face,
that explosion, and her match catches for an instant
a shape she cannot save, an eye that is

more memory than the gelatinous blue she long ago forgot
like the silky ghost of love. Is it, then, some lost gust
cracking her limbs? What marked her, entered

while the little patina of her breath was shining like ice
above the worn comforter? Is it only October's
dispassionate wind circling into her yard

and under the stars, come back as brutally clear as ever
to set the pail rattling with its gallon of darkness,
to send her out with God's name on her tongue?

Under the trees, until dawn, she will stand and not break
the stream of curses though the apples, star-bruised,
go on falling and do not kiss her goodbye.

From littered ground gnarled Winesaps have risen in drifts.
It comes, the faint sweet bloodscent of rot comes.
It is October and nothing has happened.

BETWEEN THE MOON AND THE SUN

What has happened to the stars? What thief, thin-soled
with rocks hard as seeds at flesh, has stolen them?
Surely something darker than the night,

the river shuffling aimlessly through the yawning toybox
of the universe, the cocked and stunned
right arm of the mechanical soldier,

has come red-eyed and drooling. It has happened before.

I don't mean to harp on the infinite paradoxes
there is no untangling, but why

have the stars come to rest on our feet,
on our soles bloody and crusted, those little
mouths that never speak what they meant to?

Perhaps it is only a cramp in our sleepless bellies,
the green apples we ate one hot afternoon.
The books have always warned us.

Lying awake in this moonless room
I think of stars like a crowd of pinched seeds
falling into the apples, sending little brass hooks
shooting through the white pulp.

By the time the apple's brown ache comes who will know
the stars have been stolen, who always rose
like fathers, in dignity, over the globes in the grass?

If I slide my heavy foot onto the floor, what
will fall from my chest? What will fall into my hands

heavy with the curving clarity of everything that is
not imagination and the filaments
of words charred beyond hope?

Something has happened in the black room while we were
flat on our backs trying to give birth
to the stars

and the books, in their shrouds, have slept through it.
Come to the window and I will show the world without
dreams, starless, mouthing itself, and the apples

growing black with nothing to tell us. Nothing.

WILLOWS, POND GLITTER

In the place of the drowned, above the black sheen of a pond
giving its most indifferent shrug at dusk

you have seen this, but you did not see between shadows
what it was and the reason, simple enough,
wakes you in the sowing dark

where the leaves fester in storm. On the edge
of the willows leaning together like shy schoolgirls,
the silver flank of the sunfish

in molt the color of oatmeal still arches stiff and hurls
back the hot light streaming through the heart
of hill-warped trees, hurls and twists
from each scale set into position by
secret and implacable desire

a few flowing rays of light you saw but did not name.

They follow you into the bedroom calmly swimming
in that pulse of the far off lightning.
The eye, glazed and womanly swollen, in mud

tilts now like a sinking rowboat as sheets of water climb
through willow and maple, and surely you sense
something as the nippling water sucks
down the hanging last drops on leaves.

The reason, oh it is simple enough, but you can't understand
why this small ghost
should make you want to cry out to God

16

who, at the window, you have looked for as if you believed.
You have seen me, huddled by the woodshed, my apron
held fully over my face but the light behind
coming anyway clean through.

Here I am, me, sitting down in water and afraid to cry out
what I have seen and you have seen and nobody
understands, that enormous hunger.

I swear I will come back if you can tell me what it means
to hear the world belch its ugly answers clear as the truth
a child would be too scared to lie about.

THE SOUND OF A SILK DRESS

The man with no name came,
his pants thick to the knees
with burrs, and he cradled
his face in his knuckles

and cried, if you can call
silence crying. One of us
spoke of dust on the sills
of the man's house. The lid

of light lowered, flattened,
birds darted. Across fields
the flicker of lamps began
but we stayed speaking softly

of the yellow faces of friends
in the dark, their suppers,
an empty chair. The man
backed into his steps, turned

from us, for we were not home,
kicked the dirt and then was
gone. Later we tried to name
the luck we had all had

in youth, dogs, field, love.
I remember him now walking
out of our bodies to touch
the dress with no music

in that box. I knew I would
follow him in my own time,
the dress was electric, his
knuckles white in that moon.

At the door when he comes
out of glowing stars, I say
Lord I don't know what to do
but go home, wash, and wait.

DREAMS IN SUNLIT ROOMS

A pit as black as the secret bubble of a coal lump,
geode-brilliant and shimmering
as the heart's wet valves,

where a simple bird hungry enough to eat anything
would not go: this is something like what
I woke in, and there were many

of us hugging those walls, our mouths suddenly
open as if to say what we had always meant.
I wish I could tell you it was not dawn

with the sun's pale yellow racing down, for some
cannot believe death comes in the milkman's
hour or that it is, like the wife
in her gown, sleepless, out pruning the roses

although no one is expected. Have you
thought such a place could be,

without your knowing it, just there in your yard?
I don't want to alarm you, but the shadows flickering
through the locust so the green and gray

light falls on your face, what do they mean?
And is your child only sleeping

as precise as a glass statue this glary morning?

CONVULSION

It arrives with no time to think of meaning, fever
like the bloodstreaks on the late bulbs

of wild roses there by the farm's rotting fence.
It is six-thirty and the cloudless horizon

of October hangs like a split-lipped laborer brooding
over his gun and the suddenness of his fate,

the same horizon running its moment through me, what
has happened changeless and painless as hysteria

in that empty and distant land we loved. I don't know
what is in the placid slick of your eyes

anymore, even when my hand lies down in the boiling
memory of your skin. We left you. We moved,

with dishes and debris sold, came here and no one
calls your name upstairs in the mild mean weather.

The creak and ball-bearing spin of bicycles fills
the street flaming with leaves. A cardinal jeers

for something hungrily alive in the limbs. I ask
you to think about the life we came away from

because I remember a moment I did not try to keep
which clings to me now, a time when your lips

flew apart in this violent light. Take your time.
I know you are far away and the sun is monstrous

through the slats crossed and ticked by wind
in the infinite instant that seized you.

Here they say such weather is unusual, cold and teasing
hours what we expect to get. I smile

expecting whatever comes, for the farm is far gone
and night keeps coming like the shot-to-hell look

in every face I see. Listen, I would run and never
drink another drop to hold that moment again, you

clenched and breathless in my arms as we went down
in the pond water that ballooned on your fever

before the moment came shaking me like a dog's jaws
loose from you, from the hour, from hoping.

A MEMORY AT THE EDGE OF SWOLLEN RIVERS

Her. A quick and brittle music
as of harpsichord or bare feet treading
the cold deep of holly leaves.

The bones fell out of the bag
that was her skin.

They must make a sound like a suite
in a deaf composer's ear,
that tumbling

after the rush of sleep shattered.
Who stands by the river as we
stood, afraid of our bodies,
you already aching

for what we said before the dust?
The river lapped and seemed to love
all the things we could be.

Years ago then, with a stick, I gouged
something green and she,

crying: *Let it go, it stinks.*
I teased her whom I loved, I swore
she was going to eat whatever
the river allowed us

and saw her eyes grow small and dart
in the shallows like small fish.
She gulped the river in.

It blew up her breasts that were white
with the first milk of her making.
The flood delivered her.

Below zero now, the sun dazzling snow
welds each watching eye to a slit.
Whose boy is this, whose somebody's
heart-rattling pain

goes with his stick to the waters?
I follow him and do not speak
for I would not want to have
to take that face in my hands,
wet with a green confusion.

We are all hungry, my mouth said.

Shyly, she seized my wrists, her mouth
opened to sing in a hard air,
then was gone, and all of us

with sticks trying to find her.

THE TRUE SOUND OF THE GOSHAWK

A gathering of dust, that gray piston from the world's
first balance insinuates everything and comes
down from blue-white croppings of rock
in Wyoming. Hoofprints fade, they
do not notice how they are

filled with that small body's cold summoning, but I see
that strange gesture which is like the swoop
of love, its corrective oscillations
without fear and beyond loneliness
that flies in my body and waits.

She spills over ledge-walls like sunlight and is what,
in pinion and scrub oak, alerts the curled feet
for the running dream, the zero flight
that roots in the brain and lifts
each eye at the last, impossible

instant of fear. Through memory I follow its falling
and become what I was, a child playing in dirt,
my face up and frozen enough to see a hawkish
face in that second-story window,
that brightness of flesh

already wilting as it saw what it saw and understood
the earth's blunt deliberations. And I saw
through a handful of dirt I had thrown up
only shadows, shifting particles trying
to take a shape in the air. I could hear

not even one of the wordless cries out of her dream;
saw, but could not translate that feather
flickering of her mouth, open, hungering
to lift me out of the world before
the dirt fell, slamming shut

the slits of my eyes. I saw her flinch as the shadow
came on her like a thing she had not thought
could be ours and now was. I did not know
why she cried out but began to howl
my child's tears

as if I knew what she knew, that the heart tears open
like the goshawk's mouth when it sees at last
what it has come for, but there is no cry
to outlast each cleft passage of rock
where a tongue of snow burns.

Long ago I saw that first wet glimmering of hawk tongue
and did not know, as I know now, the tiny scream
lingers only to say what has happened.
In pinion, already, eyes lift and are
too late, the heart chills and flakes.

ANTELOPE STANDING, SOME LYING

Somebody had seen them from the highway,
had slowed for the curve which did not
betray its downskidding slope
almost always, in that season,

thick with the black ice that gives nothing
the eye could whisper to the nerves.
Somebody used to them, carrying
a small wedge of salt

or maybe only some need to stop and look
into the night's moon-burnished bed.
After that he turned in sheets to say
Hundreds of them, some
down and dark as rocks.

Not saying the black eyes flared, the hooves
chipped that snow to tiny explosions.

Not saying how the sheer air knifed lungs
as he lifted face to glare at the far peak
silent as God, unreal.

But later, when night clenched around him,
when memory flashed out of shadow,
he woke certain they had called

yet lay still and dark, afraid to look
where he knew there was someone
staring from the mirror.

And remembered then his sister and mother,
in homespun cloth the color
of blue wildflowers,
climbing that hill.
They turned, they waved, so tiny—

and kept eyes closed, for he knew lying
in ice-glazed ground they were gone.

What could he say if, summoned by the dark,
he should see a room full of antelope
and himself appallingly lost
in the slick holes of their eyes?

Hundreds, just standing. I don't know why.

UNDER THE SCRUB OAK, A RED SHOE

Wrapped in a twisted brown stocking, strangled in the rolled
nylon of our grandmothers, it was wedged at the heart
of what little cool shade ever accumulated there.
You would have to walk out of your way, back
along an arroyo twisting and empty as memory, back
from the road out of town so far the sky itself
signals another world. To find it you do that,

though, in any case, you are simply walking and it appears,
something red shining through the gray-green glaze
of stunted limbs. If you were looking for a lost child,
your steps deliberate and slow, you might see it.
Otherwise you will go on. That is what we do.
But it waits to reveal itself, like an eye
in the darkness, and you may innocently look into that

moment, and may imagine why it lacks the slender heel which
must, once, have nailed many boys against a wall
where she walked. I kneel and pick it up
as you would, hearing though it is noon
the moony insects cry around her, hearing also
the nylon flake like pieces of skin against my skin,

feeling the sound of its passage from her shaven calf, a screech
like the hawk's when he is distant and not hungry.
In this arroyo no one could have seen her stop,
not as drunk as she pretended, sitting long
and, in time, methodically undressing, beyond
thinking now, placing her bundled shoe with care.
She must have been small and would have borne the usual

bruises, so we would have had no fear of any we might add,
when we stood smoking by the wall, cat-calling lightly.
It would have been one of those nights the breath
aches it is so pleased with itself, then she
appeared in that red like the first cactus buds,
something clearly wrong with her but that, by God,
no concern of any red-blooded buck she might want.
In the junk car someone squealed, some rose
and fell. There were no names. I did not mean

whatever I said, but said it because she was so small, she
could not hide her fear and shivered on her back.
Such moments we tell ourselves to walk away from,
and we do, as now I have walked in my hoping
for absence, but there is no absence, only
what waits, like this shoe, to reach, to say please
as best it can for whoever comes along, as if forgiveness
were what it meant, and love, as if any weather
that red shining endured was the bruise
you might have kissed and might not yet refuse.

Hospital Memory During Storm

for Robert and Michele DeMott

HOSPITAL MEMORY DURING STORM

1

Time ticks everywhere and the stone, water-worn, takes
your testimony of pain like a smiling mongoloid.

Waking in the midsummer violence of lightning, you
find yourself naked and in need of the woman

who softly is there where you had, an instant before,
been certain witness of a terrible death.
Passion. And later, more than half in dreaming,

you cry out to damn the gnawing hours that tear
your memory of peace. The doctor

came, antiseptic, but he could not do what was required.
What is required? Have you after all these years
come to know that in any moment? Time, all day,
ticks like the sprinkler in your garden.

2

Under tubing that hangs and shines like gravity's spillage
your son opens his mouth to scream off the dog
suddenly looming at him five floors up, a raw
hole oozing under his eye. There is glass
and you turn to it, aware low-bellied cumulus

bruises black the running hills. In the hospital
faint bells toll a time which is not time
for the ordinary child skinned by a fall

as he hurries, late and sure of your anger, toward home.
Do you see him there, in the shadow's surge?
And what are you calling as you run?

3

His mouth sucks as if it truly loves the world and you
translate that shape of terror and say it
as love, as if love had not come too late.

Where are the right words? Who hears
what you have been trying to say? Ticks, time
does, in bubbling liquid, and you are murderous

when you see in his collapsed face the human image, meaty,
and seeping so when you think of this later it seems
the instant of no time, a dead-stopped
frieze that is everything.

At the edge of a hot night something is always waiting
unfulfilled, dangerously innocent, and probably
it has been a long time since you dawdled
into the luring dark. Probably

such an occasion returns when you pick up the pebbly Gideon
like your father's, finger-reading the words,
for though you are helpless maybe it will help you
hope the world is not deadly. Think this,
for maybe it will help you, though

the child, wordless, is screaming.

4

I must tell you there is no way for clinician or artist
to draw from that room the awful pus of death. If she,
dropping into her dream beside you, has conceived
or should yet, in the festery darkness,
do so, nothing will change. Headlines

in the morning paper are early set in sterile caps
above home snapshots. This is simple evidence.
If you have not thought out these things, it is time
to recall how you first encountered hope and what
risk you took for a plunge in desire
and a father's stare straight up at the moon.

5

The world gives no guarantee but of loss and life.
Love her now, wake her and do this, though she
may be as lost to you as the redolent
flowers in the vase. Hope's hunchback
sings from her sleeping and if you
pay attention you may recall your heart's faith
before memory and the wreckage of promise.

6

Do you think it is virtue to go on grieving, to wish back

forever that breath fluttered in a cage of small bones?
You too must hurry to get home and under the black
chance of falling night. Passion,
if you once believe in it, is a way of hope.

Between her teeth a weak current of air whistles. Though
her lips are dry, clearly she is lovely and has done
no wrong thing to bring down the lightning.
I urge you to turn to her while there
is time, before the dream returns,

for there is no child to stand stone-faced in your door.

GREENHEART FERN

for H. V.

Green
as rockwalled tide pools
we remember, shifting and transposing
itself like filigreed kelp sea-blossomed
in Keatsian dark even our best dreams must envy,
a simple plant with a spare grandmotherly thirst,
unlike yours and mine. But you poured anyway,
Lord how you poured. Then you moved it,
day after day, searching for light,
tracking every glow by a sextant,
some might have supposed,
under the soft gray
of your curls.

Like you, it went on
enlarging, sluffing off the dead
sores of self, of daily usage, fabular,
doing what it could to keep alive its house.
Each window got its share of your plant's attention.
Anyone driving by would have thought some green
invasion had caught us, would have said,
against radiant glare, we must be
slithering in a tangle of our
own making, though such
green was surely
luscious.

Today,
years from those tendrils,
from your finest lacy work at life,
I entered a house whose owner keeps plants
as you would not imagine anyone decently could,
rationing water as if it were castor oil and ignoring
the yellow sere of litter. In that room dark
as a clock's heart I heard the tick
of your breath's small judgment,
and almost, as I sat in a lump,
felt those fronds turn to me,
as if seeking the hands
cold and folded
I had for a week
forgotten.

CHINABERRY TREE

It squatted in a grandmotherly yard,
surrounded by the breaking teeth
of a fence I left once
with a sheer tendril of skin.
It kept a dog whose folds of fur
held the rain and the dust
in a sweet comfort to me.
I remember falling suddenly
face to face with a creature
hidden behind its warped trunk,
her dark skirt billowing
with what must have been wind
but seemed the wild love
of an animal's shadow. She
lifted me to bed, cradling
my body like a crushed lily,
and I lay watching the tree
long after the dog disappeared
in the slow stream of the world,
long after her last steps
fled in a drift of small leaves.
This was no tree for the great
events, scarcely could sustain
the dream-weight of a boy,
and you could find scarred
in its flesh no deep initials,
but I remember its yellow berries
toppling silent and ripe,
how the day I walked out
they burst into bright tears.

These were the crushed fruit
of no worth, then as now,
clinging to the shoes
that pinched grown feet,
staining every least fabric
with that awful stink
not quite human, not of earth.

OVER THE OZARKS, BECAUSE I SAW THEM, STARS CAME

On my back, shirtless and with no friend, in September
when the time is for a young man to have seen breasts
only slightly larger than his own, thinking of her
who is inexplicably older but was not

not an hour before: to have seen that then like a purple
bruise (that strange) through the gaunt, stretched neck
loop of her T-shirt stained by wrestling, I tell
you I felt the tick of grass and itch-weight

of earth and thunderous roll of the Missouri gathering
downhill toward the ocean; and thought then, as I ate
from all silence the green bitter grapes which were
by my grandmother forbidden, being poisoned

to ward off disease from Arkansas, for the first time
that I would rather be dead than not to be alone
with what I had seen, savoring her as sunlight
curved through the grape leaf. If ever in

that bed of rocks I feared what held those hard nubs
inviolate might eat my guts out or wished some other
season, cold or wet, had kept me from the accident
of what was, I cannot recall. There was sun,

a little wind, a space of ground yellow with dandelion,
that throb of passage, fracturing shadows, grapes
with no name. Once, then, I floated in a world
I knew to be infinite, delicious, itself

churning and speaking through the voice of each shadow
and juncture of light. After that I slept, improbably
dreaming I stood in a center of light, and woke
in the dark, godless and afraid, alive.

HAWKTREE

Tonight in the hills there was a light
that leaped out of the head
and yellow longing of a young boy.
It was spring and he had walked
through the toy-littered yards
to the edge of town, and beyond.
In the tall spare shadow of a pine
he saw her standing, she of skin
whiter than the one cloud
each day loaned to the long sky,
whiter even than the pure moon.
But she would not speak to one
who kept her name to himself
when boys laughed in the courtyard.
He watched her burn like a candle
in the cathedral of needles.
After a while he saw the other light,
the sun's leveling blister, bring
its change to her wheaten hair.
In growing dark he waited, certain
she would hear the pine's whisper,
counting on nature's mediation.
But she would not speak and even
as he watched she vanished.
Slowly he knew his arms furred
with a fragrant green darkness
and as the moon cut its swaths
on the ground, as trucks rooted
along the road of colored pleasures,
he felt his feet pushing through

his shoes, his hair go sharply stiff.
He could hear her laugh, could see
her long finger loop a man's ear,
but this did not matter. Already
he felt himself sway a little
in the desert wind, in the wordless
emptied gnarling he had become.

DANDELIONS

What do you want to go back to?

If you think of it the vision comes, the day
bright as an arc welder's sizzle,

and you know the plump sound of single drops
of rain, staccato in a gutter,
don't belong. They mean another place.

The frail drift of a flute idly played
is only an illusion displaced from the other
days when, with the window open,

the river grayly hugged its hood of ice.

Therefore, you look harder for the leaves
growing silver-sided with butterflies
and some kind of animal waiting
with eyes wet and crystalline

as geodes under a flowing foot of water,

and the long white forearm of a valley declines
to a palm where the cloud's shadow floats
in the color of a lost nickel.

There is a face printed in the flesh of your thumb.

If, face down in the soft huzzahing of grasses,
you feel the earth breathe and the pulse

run time through each tendril's
coil, the itch

of unwashed children comes in a blush
before the assault of suffering.
In this moment, call out your name.

If you do this, you will have some idea of what
passes in the nervous system of dandelions
and in the eyes of love

once shocked wide in the welding sun.

THE WHITE HOLSTER

Ribbed with red glitter, those glass studs catch
and hold the early lights my mother
has raised in her longing. Her
hands waist-high cradle my one
gift, lovingly, while behind
her shapeless black suit
the shragged green
of the little cedar hides
in the brilliant blinking of bulbs.
Out of the light, in the dark crooked
arm of the stairs, I wait and want
to enter the room where she is. I am

still a child, though already I know the meaning
of snow on the high hall window, that
incessant pecking like sand
the wind whips out of darkness,
piling it up until there is
no place and no time
except for the moment
glimpsed, as through glass,
deep inside the snow-wash.
This year the tiny Jesus hangs
in a matchbox and the tree
wears raveled strips of news-
paper bearing names of the dead.
My naked feet slide on cold wood,
I feel my way down the dark,
for I do not want to hurry

to find her in the middle of that instant ice-
bright and all there will be of Christmas.
Long ago she called but I dawdled
in my bed to see how thin was
the white bulk of breath,
wanting and not wanting
to know how poor we had become
with a war raging and a father gone.
By each step I have grown larger
in her waiting, but am still
only a boy with no gift
except words

that, in memory, bristle and are evergreen as light
from a sparse bush she hacked and stood up
that night. I give them back now,
remembering how long it takes
to come into this loving

room where she stands for me,
her face, in sepia, slightly bent
over the white holster. The gun
suddenly silvers like a long stroke
of whirled snow before her body
and I see, now, she holds
my gift, the leather
stiff and white, the red tears
of glass, the black fake fur
in tufts making a pony's shape.
Her arms, light-bruised, extend

as if from the cedar's delicate, bent spine,
its fur and her dress one dark
blinking, as now my eyes open
and shut on that image. Words
fill that room with the rush
of needles gone crisp in time.
They sweep me into her arms,
words that lace the dark memory
of joy to the particular glint
of her hand on my hair. *It is
what you wanted isn't it. He said
in his last letter you would want it.*

Overhead tonight, in snowless December,
the stars blink quiet explosions.
Their bursts fall endlessly
on shoulders of rock and skirts
of cedar, until there is no square
inch of earth that does not gleam.
At stair top, with hand flat
on the wall, switch off now
so the tree squats alone,
I remember the long light
pooled on the floor,
that flesh and black suit
I must come down to.
All day I will draw guns,
deep in a child's joy,
shaking the cedar like a bomb.
Happy, I will shoot at her, *happy,*

until at last the words bang
from her mouth as she holds me,
saying *yes, yes, yes.*

HATH THE DROWNED NOTHING TO DREAM?

Among milkweed, in the wide-shaking wind
that unlocks each eye, the carpenter
stops, his board balanced
on his shoulders. Something triggers

the river light on the underedge of leaves,
the flat ringing of helpers' hammers
looms in delicate song. The term
of his mourning circles back

on itself. *Hey,* he shouts to the roofers.
Her hair is in his eyes, its falling
at her waist in starlight, music
he suddenly begins to dance to

as if it were not that black force pooling
under the C & O slag heap, not the dream
murderous among the crickets where
she, so long, had lain

humming in his ear. The glint in the green
is like wedding silver flushed
from mud and roots, and it clicks
for that first usage — his ear

lives again and immediately the board whirls.
Out of the darkened eye of the earth
he becomes the dreamed self rising
back to life and the moment

spreads into the shadowy faces of helpers.
On roofs, under timbers, out of trucks
they see the miracle of absurd light
spinning from his body

and there is not anything to keep off now
their need to leap up from the nails,
to cry back *Hey*, though each one
tomorrow will not remember.

And he, when he falls dizzied and sinking,
will think it was only a dream that,
in the long madness of labor,
would be heart-breaking if it lasted.

THE COLLECTOR OF THE SUN

Through the small door of a hut
he stares at us, our movements,
the thousands of faces we are,
the booming world's roar

that, later, for a drifting instant,
he will enter. His extra shirt
tied by its arms for a sack,
he will be lost in his luck.

By the freeway, whipped as a weed,
he stalks the malignant ground
for bottles, and we wear on.
He doesn't imagine anyone

weeping in anger as he looms up.
And when he comes to the truck
parked, the woman asleep inside,
he thinks of his nights, wide

as the blue glare on the concrete,
full of glass and the clink-clink
of his business. For him sunset
is the good hour, the shapeless

beams of headlights always thick,
blending with sun to flick
off what he hunts. He is alone,
himself, dreaming of the blown

treasures of the world, the bottles
like loaves of gold. The rubble
of everything falls about him
like snow. He bends, reaches, grins,

and ignores whatever we scream.
His tarpaper walls are the dream
he has given himself. At night
a wind plays over the pipes

he has fashioned from glassy mouths.
The world seems right, as he lies out
in bed, but fingers itch, and a face,
oh whose is it, leans, leans like grace

and he can't remember whose or why.
At dawn, aching, he watches the sky,
sees dark birds pass, then us,
and is himself again, staring, blessed.

SEA CHANGE: THE RENTED HOUSE
AT SEAL ROCK, OREGON

Mercifully, the sun spangles on the tile and on
my closed eyes, spilling that unlooked for
and dusky forgiveness which fog, for days,
denied us. I roll myself in the sheets,

trying to come up out of the blindness of a dream's
drift and whirl. I can hear gulls and children
far off, blooming, the world I walked away
from years ago, but I am not the one

walking out of the surf. Somehow I have slipped,
like the seal, down into the root-tangles
of dream. Phosphorous rocks loom and glitter
above me, breaking the sun in pieces

each with the shape of those I've loved and mourned.
With them I want to give up exile and rise
in their gold looming, seeing at last
how they hope for this to happen,

so cry out and become a child who discovers himself
alone in the house for the first time.
I fling my small sounds against the walls
where parents were, just now, and try

to beg back everything that, slowly, has been moving
off into the shadows of the rocks. Like you
I have found myself where I never was, dream-
drowning and entering the memory

of all cries made by the sudden cramp of love,
feeling my heart swell against each rib
of a remembered light. In this room
and in the fusing eyeblink of morning

I roll and make the cries until her face finds me, finds
my lips cool in the delicate hair on her neck.
This is what I have waited for, the body
of joy buoyant with forgiveness, all

bodies seal-sleek rising from the fracturing waters.

RAIN FOREST

The green mothering of moss knits shadow and light,
silence and call of each least bird where
we walk and find there are only a few words
we want to say: water, root, light, and love,
like the names of time. Stunned from ourselves,
we are at tour's tail end, our guide long gone,
dawdling deep in what cannot be by any human
invented, a few square miles of the concentric
universe intricate as the whorls of fingertips.
The frailest twigs puff and flag in the giantism
of this elaborate grotto, and we are the dream,
before we know better, of an old grotesque
stonecutter who squats under a brow of sweat,
the afternoon a long glowing stalk of marble.
We have entered the huge inward drift behind
his eyes and wait to become ourselves. We stare
through limpid eyes into the vapor-lit past
where breath, wordlessly, like a near river
seams up, seams in and out and around darkness.
Somewhere far back in the hunch of shadows,
we stood by this wall of vines, and he, angry,
froze us in our tracks and the blade of belief.
That tree there bore the same long slithering
of light from a sky he owned. Disfigured now,
its trunk rises thick and black as a monument
that rings when struck. Here the hiking path,
a crease, stops, then spirals around into stumps.
Our party has gone that way, stumbling quietly.
From time to time, someone calls out but we know
only the words whispered from the wall of leaves:

water, root, light, and love. We stand silent
in the earliest air remembered, hearing at last
the distant and precise taps of the mallet
until our clothes, as if rotted, fall away
and the feckless light fixes us on the column
of our spines. Without warning, we begin to dance,
a bird cries, and another. Our feet seem to spark
on the hard dirt as we go round the black tree
and for no reason we know we see ourselves
throwing our heads back to laugh, our gums
and teeth shiny as cut wood, our eyes marbled,
straining to see where it comes from, that
hoarse rasp of joy, that clapping of hands
before which we may not speak or sing or ever stop.

Settlement

for Norman and Jody Dubie

For after all, a gale of wind, the thing of
mighty sound, is inarticulate. It is a man who,
in chance phrase, interprets the elemental
passion of his enemy. Thus there is another
gale in my memory, a thing of endless, deep,
humming roar, moonlight, and a spoken sentence.
Joseph Conrad

The vision of dreams is this against that,
the likeness of a face confronting a face.
Sirach 34:1-3

SETTLEMENT

Wind lifted the curtains and I saw how far
it had come to enter my dream
of the story she was telling.
Out of the brown distant
mountains, from grassy shadows,
farther than I had ever been,
it came and lay nudging
the scrolled, hand-stitched
linen hung by her mother
over logs, then these windows.

She did not tell me about desert wind or
why she had to take me back
through her gathering of dreams,
the stained faces, hands no more
to me than iced footsteps
left in the winter.
Now, in my own overheated room,
the grease-flecked plates
wait to be stacked and I
sit by myself and begin to know
they memorized me and took me
into the lost black
geographies of their bodies.

They were poor, they ate whatever might be
found, wormy bread, sometimes the dead
worms burrowed in a green crust.
That room was big, though spare,
dark molding whose varnished

promise had long ago spidered
still gleamed like a cave's
footpath where I was
summoned, small and cold
in my swallowing
against the clear early light.

In one corner of the airy room she is rocking,
fawn hair gone gray in slight drifts.
Her legs cross at ankles, housed
in the anonymous black skirt.
Her blouse hangs ice-white
as snow curved, sometimes,
against the leaded glass.
The rug, red but with deep blue
curlicues of wool, betrays
the worn tread of boots
to the squat stove.

Today it is August, so hot
breath waits in the mouth.
She has been reading for hours
but, now, at some passage, stops,
her forehead damply beaded, to tell me
Books are all lies and no help.
A chestnut colt throws its voice
against the barked corral that will,
before the first snow, collapse.
The great book falls from her lap
with the popped sound of flesh

struck, and I know it means
she has fallen into the rooms
of the old people lost
in house dust and yellower than paper.
We have sure God seen bad times.

The book, in my memory, is like her
judgment but was no more than
a small roof splayed over no walls
like the useless napkin on my plate.
It was a world of glorious stories
with horses like the two
thick-coats her father left us
and men who did not choose
the swords that cleaved joy
like my own Wyoming stars.
Loyalty was a thing I understood
as she twisted me through words
plain as that open room.

She did not tell me how they passed into
the settlement of dust always
weaving through the windows
to dull the flash of uncut hair,
how the portrait of our ancestor,
in tunic and empty scabbard,
unjeweled, would go on
flaking around the painted
blue shock in the eye holes.
But with crash of steel

that face would swing
down a hillside she made
enormous and green until
I stared into the horizon
where I might someday cling
to a nag's mane in small glory.

Let us pray. And I would squint, not wanting to leave
all the light, as her prayer mumbled
backward crazily to freeze a man
who led a mule and a broken mare
through the nightpaths, moonless,
over the Shenandoah fieldstone, not
stopping for fear of deserter's rope,
into blistering miles of light
already our memory. No more
than a shrug of his meaningless
thrust into history, she
prays him, or someone like him,
to forgive her despair, tears
on her cheek and on mine
the same bright, last glimmer
rising from these leftovers at dusk.

Outside the wind grinds leaves in the street,
leaves face to face tumbling,
clinging for an instant
and I am afraid I cannot well
remember her rough palms deeply
stained by the ground I loved,

but remember the crow-darting
of her eyes, the vision
of a man with a woman, both
in fear on the moonscape of prairie,
mouths wide to sing as they
scoured with sand the cache
of pewter plates. Fire-flare,
for a while, defined them

as I, in my mind, am defined by a moment. I
stood, not only in my own body, but
armored by dream and glow of noon
in an arroyo fleshed with first
gaudy flowers of cactus, and knew
in the midst of cavalry charge,
imagined, the green odor of
water. It was, suddenly, there—
the speech of the world—
it cried out *Believe!* I did,
and did not think how she,
at window, would have seen
the sun withering all
I loved beyond image or word.
In that moment, I think, I felt
the tuned, single sway of prayer

trying to pass through the curtain of my skin.
I ran through the gouged trench,
certain snakes skittered before
the sun-burst of my toy pistol,

until I rested at the flume
end of rocks, ashen, and
then climbed on a nag, cataracted
and stolid, to kick his laboring
ribs until they bled. My heart,
in joy, beat without effort,
as I roared in significant battle
against myself and the scar
of our house, white in that place.
The goshawk rolled overhead
as if he knew the carrion
I would leave. Later I sat
on the wooden circle of rails
to see him bend the air,

ruthless in his unwill, as tonight I sit in words
plummeting down through my head
to enter again the room
where my mother is trying
to lay out the act of settlement.
But cannot get there, quite, for
I have only left the corral's height
to lean on my grandfather's last
post whose nail, raw and thick,
waits still to be struck, and sings,
sometimes, in the nightwind.
From here I see the window,
the wing of the chair,
but no face over the red and blue
rug like a desert orchid, no
hands translucent

that must come down on me like a hawk's shuddering
all the way through my wingblades
for what I have done, no man
yet, though man-tall and cruel.
Here I remember the knight,
the story beginning everywhere,
words wandering in frail paths
full of campfires and droppings
of ghostly horses. A queen's crowned
bones glow from her face, and soon
a castle, clammy, will rise,
a crumpling oak fire inside,
and downhill a shady village.
The stone floor is mantled
by knight's boon, a rug
whose creatures livingly weave

what I most understand, the shelter and sacrament
that makes her voice keen and tingle
like an antelope's as she dives
under the dark's shoulder. Gray,
in quick glints like a goshawk,
the man comes, leans, kisses
her forehead. Then
I am born. Then the man,
like a thought, breaks or leaves,
and we are alone in the dust
of words, fingers racing the lines
as if, sun-blind, we have come
at last to the last rock

and the level horizon red, now,
as her handprint on my flesh
that has settled deeply in—

Why do you do it? I sit toying with a knife
in the food I do not want, trying
to answer, but lost as always
in the bright bloom of cactus,
in the surprise I take
from the flanks of a blind horse
whose knifing squeal rides
up my arm like joy's word,
only it is not, and the blood,
like grease, scabs my touch
until I do not know what
I believe or believed—
but know her voice licking out
in hawk shadow to snag,
like a nail, whoever might
pass in the arrogance of dream.
*Well, what have you learned
in your god-blessed wandering?*

At the end must life seem so unreasonable,
the hawk's screech faint as snow-rasp,
coal's soft inward settling
that leaves the armored stove
empty, the room dusted blue?
I went in the world and she
remained in that place

where I had grown to no answer,
our lessons unfinished.
But received, in time, the summons,
mailed by a man who wandered,
they said, but good with a hammer.
I went too late. The house
stunk like a hut so I lunged
angrily at the swollen window,
the rooted frame refusing, and
burst elbows through glass.
The few drops on the rug,
long-ragged, went brown.

I sat in her rickety chair and, for a time,
slept, and no dreams. Then woke
cold, cramped. She had
no wood now and no coal.
I took up the tattering blue book,
making a fire of its pages,
clawing them out, only the sewn
and deepest still whole,
the rest shriveled and sere.
I had not thought to bring food
so drank the gin quickly,
not a word spoken. Then wind,
with the light scent of—was it
cactus?—came, and I dreamed
a far cleft of rock, a man
trying to pull something
from the darkness of stone.

I woke in the memory
of weaving fingers,
the cathedral, that whistling

when the world stared in its empty abstraction
and terror, what she taught me.
I had been afraid one night,
sleepless in the grave desert
that stalked each window.
She had climbed the black stairs,
calling ahead to comfort me,
and in dead dark, bookless,
made each sound of each animal
the knight kept alive in his
rug and the house of his heart.
I blew hard for that music
but tucked my cold hands
under armpits and listened
all night to the rattle of glass
like teeth, to an agitation
of wind at our door

that was, perhaps, only the boiling of dust
and lopsided hilling of the world's
words—all she had left me,
as now the leaves outside scrape
in a language I almost understand,
the night-splintered whisper
of longing. Is that it? Almost
I hear a man and a woman

speak to me from far back,
offering words like fire-sizzled
chunks of meat to one hovering
in darkness, a glint only.
I do not know what they mean
but take what is given now
without judgment or promise,
letting it whistle up
whatever shape or shade of love
the wind will settle on me.

And now I think of that curtain lying
like a skin between my body
and all the world.
I think of the man with a hammer
tapping down the dark
blinding boards, as leaves,
this night and every night,
nail against my window
their decomposing palms.
For this and the words for this
she prayed, and I will pray
that all remain what it has been
in communion of dream, except
for the scummed eye
that horse turned on me
as if he who could not forgive,
forgave—knowing I would
ride him forever,
knowing the endless, indivisible

miracle we were in that place
would be unspeakable as a wind
in the throat's deep
where it is.

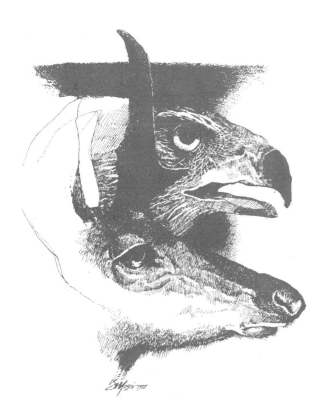

WAKING AMONG HORSES

So then in the morning we would wake,
the steam of summer on us,
sheets kicked back,
and out of whatever dream
we had been floating through
our mouths would open and lazily
cup the air as if it were forever
the water of love's sailing,
and it would begin again.

Your hair in my hand drifting,
the dark odor of pine pitch, that
silent sizzle of light on our skin
would return, would be the bell
and curve of your breast, sudden,
then the slow saw droning
each of its brassy teeth
over the distances of water.
We would see the child—
almost—that face we tried
to conceive out of the instant
before time sent the sound
of labor's breaking,

and I would ask what face you had seen,
in this birth of the imagination,
until you would cry no, no,
until the dream we rode
like a farmer's horse
became two and we would fall,

whoever we were, staring
through the tiny attic window
at the blue emptiness where
birds jeered their confusion.

So we would lie in the split vision
of that moment which is everything
memory gives us, trying to know
the nature of love, hearing
it begin with the horses
in the near fields of June,
hearing their naked whistle
like startled upriding
birds, not knowing
where, in what swoop of joy,
we might rise or land or what
hardness, again, was beginning.

IN THE YARD, LATE SUMMER

In the yard the plum tree, wild
with a late summer wind,
shakes its thousand planets
of sweet flesh.
Does it mean to resist
this gush that drops
one order of things
into another? It keels,
leaning at forces we can't
see, can't know the edge of.
Its memory keeps only two
commands: this lives, this
dies from the licking sun.
There is no metaphor
to reveal what it has known
in its brooding years.
We watch the purple fruit fall
as leaves shear and snap
and nail themselves to light.
Between us the wind
is a word seeking a shape,
hovering in passion
and risen from the ground
of memory clenched
in roots and long tendrils.
Hearing that, knowing ourselves
wingless and bestial, we wait
for the sun to blow out,
for the return of that first
morning of pink blossoms

when we saw the dark stains
of our feet printing
what we were on that
dew-bed of the world.
The tree, too, waits
in its old unraveling
toward a naked silence,
its language wild and shocked.

THAT MOMENT, WHICH YOU COULD LOVE, WHAT OF IT

Today, bitch of a day, trembling
false light on everything,
the promised change
is not: dusk rounds corners,
a newspaper under its arm, gray
overcoat flapping, one thing
to count on beside self's sickness,

snow remembered foul with ice,
hunched in the aborted grass
like terror, one snaking
tongue flares in a small bush
lost in winter. You try, can't
hold it. The window's iced.

Hold still now: the diva
no one ever expects comes
into your room, hanging
plants rustle, coilings, tendrils
almost music; the aquarium bubbles
with biting shadows, rhythmic
wakes, and still her voice

breaks with static, she goes.
On the table the hulls of salt
and pepper shakers, tracks
in what you poured out
circling on themselves, playfully
at first, then desperate for what
was the beginning: suddenly

the fierce blaze of light, her
cry riding the one long note
of your breath, the overcoat
left in a corner, and you
know a surge in the earth,
something trackless, nor of wires
received, envelops you, is

and is gone with the shift she
rides, the beautiful diva
straining notes like moments
so rare nothing dies. Who
would not risk everything
for this, even as darkness rushes
over the fish, the salt, the snow?

BLACK WIDOW

I imagine her trying, trying to catch it. First,
dusting dutifully, slow now for the child
leans heavily under her dress, she finds
the web behind her hand-loom. Her frail
hands mean to weave a birth cloth, but time
has speeded up on her. On her face, the worst

black shadow crawls and squats and waits. At last,
delicately, she moves the loom to discovery.
The black spot hunches in the black heart
of the corner, snoozing in maternal reverie.
Her hands, now, shake. The web gleams like art.
She feels heavier, her fast blood slows to paste.

An hour later, pulse loud as a truck, she kneels
with the glass jar and strikes out at it.
Legs black as a satin dinner dress uncoil
and dance her back in memory to moves quick
still in her body. Clumsy, afraid, she fails
the first time, then screws tight the metal seal,

but punches a small hole for air. All afternoon
she keeps it in the refrigerator, admiring
that red jewel she cannot bear to smash.
Home from work, a husband, I find the thing
is mine to kill, like memory. She won't watch.
In the yard the sun boils, the sky is sheer blue.

I tell her it is a small thing she must put away
like clothing in a cardboard box. I hold her,
driven to distance by the swollen bulb
of her womb, but she cries and shivers.
At night she wakes from dreams of a world
shatteringly bright and of her girlish waist

gone, with my foot on it like an executioner. She
swears she's full of spiders, still half
asleep, and kicks the blankets off to lie
naked in a little light like an hourglass.
Accused, I sink in my own dark, the itch-glide
on my skin the fear of what she bears and flees.

TREEHOUSE

Under the pitched roof
of a single leaf
I have come to
the forgiving place
my body may hide in.
The rain speaks
its soft German
through a frayed
bronze moustache
whose wings,
when I arrive
and am still,
quiver into an end-
less angling of stories.
My father, that sobbing
inventor of all,
has come out
from under the gray
wheezing house-pipes,
the mud of his plumbing
quick with rain.
Guttural as a tyrant,
he pulls down
each leaf's lovely
palm and cups me
into a floorless room.
Through each stem-neck
and tongue of vein,
he sings at the world's
outrageous heart,

that accuser,
to whom we are
the inexplicable things,
the loved debris.

WAVING

In the backyard, by the stilled
oscillations of the cheap
metal fence defined
by the weight of children,
the small maple
waves in the first
gusts of a fall day.
Behind breath-frosted
glass, hearing far off
my child's cry, I
see this waving become
my father's thick arms.
He waves at the ball game
where players swarm
at his call. One spits.
He waves from the nose
of a rowboat, drunk
with fish and ashamed.
He waves at the black
end of a treeless street
where my mother has turned
from the house, crying.
He waves on a little hill
above the playground,
his whistle shearing
over each knuckle
of asphalt. When I stop
running, out of breath,
he is still there, waving,
and I am waving, beating

the air with my arms,
sored and afraid,
and there is no wind, only
the brilliant distance
like a fence between us,
waving and waving.

AUGUST, ON THE RENTED FARM

In this season, through the clear tears
of discovery, my son calls me
to an abandoned barn. Among
spiders' goldspinning and the small
eulogies of crickets, he has entered
the showering secret of our lives,
and the light fur of something
half-eaten mats his hands.
Later, on a rotting length
of pine, we sit
under the star-brilliance
of swallows fretting
the hollow light.
Under them, dreamless,
we have come to cast
our lot with their songs
of celebration.
All afternoon we sit and become
lovers, his hand in mine
like a bird's delicate wing.
Everywhere the sparrows go down
to the river for the sweet
tears of communion. Soon,
in the yellow last light,
we will begin again to speak
of that light in the house
that is not ours, that is only
what we come to out of the fields
in the slow-plunging knowledge
of words trying to find a way home.

PLAYING BALL

Last year there was no chance.
You stared into the empty
blue as if into a room
you were afraid to enter.
So we begin, in a tangle
of absences, to know
the shapes that wait for us.
Now alone in the grass
gone green only for us,
I wave you away, seeking
the right distance until
somehow you understand and go
and are there, yourself—
that I remember and turn
away from for the first time.
These strokes are easy,
just enough to make rise
the thing you will lose
in sunlight and in fear.
I watch how you tumble
toward me, the tattering
glove of your fathers
too large, your face opening
at that deceit and the earth's
unpredictable, quick skid.
A mockingbird sits on a bench
to scout whatever moves.
He catches more than you do
but has nothing to say,
having no chance to become

the beautiful secret thing
you are, calling for more
in the high hard sun.

A MOMENT OF SMALL PILLAGERS

That flock of starlings hewing the air
above the orchard is nothing
but the strangling of desire.
I know their country is nowhere
and would not throw a single stone
against such beautiful longing.
They have walked out to be
at the heart of our bodies
and cannot find what they want,
or even a gleam from the gone sun.
Under them I bend down quietly
and pick up a black feather
as if it were the dropped scarf
of my sleeping daughter. Holding
this for hours, I find myself
unable to say a simple word
true or false, until I become
the little thing my body is
in the hiding fur of a woods.
Then I look across the hedgerows
at the foreign light of my house.
Somewhere in the distance of dark
a voice is calling my name,
but not too loud, and I want
to fly up and gather the last
radiance of the sun and take it
like a song down to her mouth.
Oh daughter, in the thick trees
where fruit bruises beyond joy,
I hunch among the starlings,

folding and unfolding my love,
afraid for the black wing of silence,
for what must wake in each voice
when it swirls up at daybreak
so naked, so uncertain, so lost.

THE DARK EYES OF DAUGHTERS

Flying from the end of my
boot, my daughter's cat,
and the tame quail gone
up in a spatter of feathers,
to leave me turning there
as the dew dulls out, bare
shoulders flushed from that
quick sprint, the back door
still banging like a ripped
shred of memory. I think
I can hear the world grind.
Like a man in a car
that's just dropped something
to howl down a quiet street,
I am saying *Please, please*
and only mean I want to
go on wherever I am going,
and want the trees to remain
a close, shadowing green
tunnel without that light
banging hard overhead and
do not want, for God's sake,
to hear this slow gouging
of sparks that is the world,
the intense unloosening stare
in the cat's eyes as I loom
out of the sudden stillness,
the fixed and heart-dark
pupils of the child startled
to see what cruelty is, always

to know this first dream of
love's division. I am crying
Please, oh, please —not
wanting this to happen, this
sun the color of a cat to fall
on her struck face that is
learning to mouth these words
without end, with only
a beginning already long lost
like pawprint or feather
where grass goes stunningly
dead, and sun, like flint, strikes.

THESE PROMISES, THESE LOST, IN SLEEP
REMAIN TO US

Night-black in the yard begins to glow, then shakes
the oaks heavy in sleep like an old dog's thighs.
This wakes a bird whose belligerent advance up limbs
reshapes the world we have known. His notes announce
what was left the day before, tricycle, toy, tree,
the newsworthy unchanged. Assiduously he sings
to make things so. He names. Hearing him, I break
from my bed of dark anxiety and the dream of a girl
sobbing at dusk for a favorite stone she's lost.
Like him, cries were all she had to summon back
her piece of the world. The scene replays and I see
I followed her up stairs, promising it all intact,
and lay me down on the toy-littered stage for prayer.

It's there I return at first light, and heavily wait.
The bird, encouraged by his story, tells another
louder than the first, making her bear blue-eyed,
bringing the breath of day to jingle her hung puppet.
He makes the dark retreat in every room, a sad light
ring the halls, as if he were meaning's journalist.
I, on the floor, lie listening, stone-numb, and ache
at every inflexible angle of being, unable to rise,
hopelessly beyond any whistling I made in the dark,
more and less than song, for her. He pursues his work,
outlining house and car, alley and insomniac. This
chatter is what it takes. I watch her face float up,
bright, round as truth itself. Light's here, known.
The news goes on, her cat's at the door and mews,
dusk's color, a garbler at best, his intention unclear.

She leaps me by a yard, is gone, a far door slamming,
out into the somewhere of the grass, defining the fur
of a cat while I count what I'd gathered in her sleep:
a small kingdom of stones. All morning I think of her,
of rooms she cracks through like light and the gleaming
ground she sifts not for the lost but the not found.
And think, too, of the bird hunkered in green shadow
and silent, concocting words for a world full of cats.
Note by note by note we arrange what's known for song
while trees tower over us, spreading a storied gray-
gold that keeps what must be found, lost, and found.
At dusk I throw the stones back in the yard. The bird
makes his inventory, the oaks yawn and settle like saints.
All night stones glow like eyes, or like nothing
we could dream, unnamed, each a promise we must keep.

The Roundhouse Voices

in memory of Ralph G. Smith and Lloyd Cornwell

THE ROUNDHOUSE VOICES

In full glare of sunlight I came here, man-tall but thin
as a pinstripe, and stood outside the rusted fence
with its crown of iron thorns while
the soot cut into our lungs with tiny diamonds.
I walked through houses with my grain-lovely slugger
from Louisville that my uncle bought and stood
in the sun that made its glove soft on my hand
until I saw my chance to crawl under and get past
anyone who would demand a badge and a name.

The guard hollered that I could get the hell from there quick
when I popped in his face like a thief. All I ever wanted
to steal was life and you can't get that easy
in the grind of a railyard. *You can't catch me
lardass, I can go left or right good as the Mick,*
I hummed to him, holding my slugger by the neck
for a bunt laid smooth where the coal cars
jerked and let me pass between tracks
until, in a slide on ash, I fell safe and heard
the wheeze of his words: *Who the hell are you, kid?*

I hear them again tonight Uncle, hard as big brakeshoes,
when I lean over your face in the box of silk. The years
you spent hobbling from room to room alone crawl
up my legs and turn this house to another
house, round and black as defeat, where slugging
comes easy when you whip the gray softball over
the glass diesel globe. Footsteps thump on the stairs
like that fat ball against bricks and when I miss
I hear you warn me to watch the timing, to keep
my eyes on your hand and forget the fence,

99

hearing also that other voice that keeps me out and away
from you on a day worth playing good ball. Hearing
Who the hell . . . I see myself, like a burning speck
of cinder come down the hill and through a tunnel
of porches like stands, running on deep ash,
and I give him the finger, whose face still gleams
clear as a B & O headlight, just to make him get up
and chase me into a dream of scoring at your feet.
At Christmas that guard staggered home sobbing,
the thing in his chest tight as a torque wrench.
In the summer I did not have to run and now

who is the one who dreams of a drink as he leans over
tools you kept bright as a first-girl's promise? I
have no one to run from or to, nobody to give
my finger to as I steal his peace. Uncle, the light
bleeds on your gray face like the high barbed wire
shadows I had to get through and maybe you don't remember
you said to come back, to wait and you'd show me
the right way to take a hard pitch
in the sun that shudders on the ready man. I'm here

though this is a day I did not want to see. In the roundhouse
the rasp and heel-click of compressors is still,
soot lies deep in every greasy fingerprint.
I called you from the pits and you did not come up
and I felt the fear when I stood on the tracks
that are like stars which never lead us
into any kind of light and I don't know who'll
tell me now when the guard sticks his blind snoot

between us: take off and beat the bastard out.
Can you hear him over the yard, grabbing his chest,
cry out *Who the goddamn hell are you, kid?*

I gave him every name in the book, Uncle, but he caught us
and what good did all those hours of coaching do?
You lie on your back, eyeless forever, and I think
how once I climbed to the top of a diesel and stared
into that gray roundhouse glass where, in anger,
you threw up the ball and made a star
to swear at greater than the Mick ever dreamed.
It has been years but now I know what followed there
every morning the sun came up, not light
but the puffing bad-bellied light of words.

All day I have held your hand, trying to say back that life,
to get under that fence with words I lined
and linked up and steamed into a cold room
where the illusion of hope means skin torn in boxes
of tools. The footsteps come pounding into words
and even the finger I give death is words
that won't let us be what we wanted, each one
chasing and being chased by dreams in a dark place.
Words are all we ever were and they did us
no damn good. Do you hear that?

Do you hear the words that, in oiled gravel, you gave me
when you set my feet in the right stance to swing?
They are coal-hard and they come in wings
and loops like despair not even the Mick

could knock out of this room, words softer
than the centers of hearts in guards or uncles,
words skinned and numbed by too many bricks.
I have had enough of them and bring them back here
where the tick and creak of everything dies
in your tiny starlight and I stand down
on my knees to cry, *Who the hell are you, kid?*

THE SUICIDE EATERS
—*poems after* Wisconsin Death Trip, *by Michael Lesy*

1. The Suicide Eater

> "G. Drinkwine, father of Miss Lillian
> Drinkwine, who committed suicide a
> few days ago, attempted suicide at
> Sparta. He swallowed a large quantity
> of cigar stubs."

Someone came to the door
asking what we are
in this world
for: a religious question,
a sequence of syllables
sing-songy really,
not the kind of thing
a man wants to answer
only days after the dirt
of his daughter's going
remains on his boots.
But those sounds whirled
on for days, like sparrows
getting up over here, sitting
down unequivocally somewhere,
and what sense in that?
I watched them many times
from the sun in her room
and no answer. Some
order is all I guessed,
maybe fright. Maybe.

You cannot eat death.
It isn't real, is it?
I called to the stranger.
I was smoking a cigar.
It was real, but it went
out: a plant raised up
in death, then dead
itself, but organized,
useful, its smoke more
tangible than words until
it died. Brown and slimy
and soft in its stink,
I broke it like bread.
Death, like life, creates
its own hunger. I had
to have more, to go on,
to feed. Understandably
there is pain in this,
maybe sickness, but words,
they are the black strangers,
unanswered, inedible.

2. On the Limits of Resurrection

> *"Christ Wold, a farmer near Poskin Lake,*
> *committed suicide by deliberately blowing*
> *off his head with dynamite. He placed a*
> *quantity of the explosive in a hole in the*
> *ground, laid his head over it and touched*
> *off the fuse exclaiming 'Here I go and the*
> *Lord go with me.' "*

After some years of my clearest testimony
I, for one, remain convinced
that in the readily-available-to-the-tactile
senses (barn reek, green moss in blue river ice,
owls like nuns after the copulating cats, etc.)
what speaks plainest is the most mysterious.

My friends in Moss Bones's beer hall (that being
his honest-to-God name) used to go home
with me and I would drag my feet
in the black locust groves
where we had all grown up pricked and bleeding.
My idea was the wind sang the truth there,
fretting the thorns like a fiddler.
If children threw stones at us I said
let them go. One drowned running away.

This year I consumed only cabbage and spring water.
The priest stepped from behind a hedgerow
in December, stinking and thundering

that he was reality (Look at me, he shouted. Look
how my body makes prints in the snow!) but I
saw beyond his foolishness. I heard owls
blaspheming the language of stones.

One day coming home, I said there is nothing else to do,
I will have to get down among the huddled things
and make a noise to get their attention.
I saw also the only woman I have ever loved
crossing the ridge, visible and silent as a stump.
Then I began to dig and I could hear dear dead mother
padding down the hall, the fat nun knocking
the river riding the bones of that child.

3. Song of the Dutch Insult

"Abraham Zweekbaum of the town of Holland
committed suicide by battering himself on
the head with a hammer."

First, I found myself kneeling
at the front steps which, blasted by sun,
cracked like the sparrow dung. In need
of fresh paint. I put out my tongue
and missed, striking my nose.
Nose took many smart blows.

Painful, of course, but it did not serve.

So, with my arm and my good hammer,
I struck at my forehead, that harborer
of various offenders. Lifting my arm for fair,
by God I hammered at the gates in the air,
grew moist with sweat, and more.
I opened a door.

My kin will tell you I was not one to swerve.

The day began with a vision over my bed, a glow
perhaps no more than a trick of light,
for I had not slept since I caught
the drifter and my wife, legs and all,
where the blackberries plumped.
Then the bird flew in, wild at my wall.

There are many ways to die and one is in the nerve.

As I have said, the nose went first.
An eye closed, more in sympathy than hurt.
Between the beginning and the end, life
demands forgiveness. I had nailed
a dark thing deeply in. Therefore,
I kneeled to peel the coffin's lid
and prayed to God to save my wife.

4. A Fixation with Birds

> "Mrs. Anna Ross, a Marquette widow, went
> insane over religion. A Chicago revivalist
> representing Dowie faith healing meetings
> there made an attempt to cure Mrs. Ross of
> lameness. Prayer was tried at several
> meetings and the final result of it was
> insanity for the woman."

The first owl appeared
as the leaves turned,
scarcely a shadow
where I lay in my bed.
The nuns had come, gone,
shaking their heads, my
hell signed and sealed.
I denounced each one,
for they had married
God, though they had
the flesh never rent
by any man. Whereas, so
I swore, I was the bride
bruited for her deeds
of sin, but cleansed, thus
as holy as the rain.
The Baptists agreed.
The Dowie man came.

By winter all the owls
were white with coals

for eyes and talons
pearl-scaled. I told
them of gentle Abraham,
my husband, the blood
we shed that first night.
Without love, how stand
in the wingless world?
The owls cooed for hours.
The Baptists prayed, oh
they dripped the water,
but in the end went.
Lame, I limped from
wall to wall and named
each owl I nailed up.

Let me not see the spring
come again, I begged.
Veins flamed my legs.
The Dowie man screamed
"Get thee gone." I did.
Dear Abraham, I cried.
They sealed my doors
and fed me gruel.
Hawks came, and kestrels,
ravens, magpies, crows,
wheeling like fools.
But I was gone, my
wings thickened white.
I ate myself sore
and the world was good.

CORNER ROOM, HOG-SCALD IN THE AIR

This is the room where she sickened, the clotted wads of paper.
The smell is that of no-smell or, more precisely, a smell
from the ancestral memory of hair dissolving.

The walls lean down with an absence like an envelope ripped.
The bedsheets lie wrinkled and twisted, but no
blanket, none needed even this near winter.

Someone has left a shoe canted at the dark woodwork, a boot
badly scuffed, its tongue out, no lace.

Only hours ago I stood at these curtains and could not think
what good they did on this poor earth where she slept
in her small frame, where now blade of light
comes in clean and is all

the world offers in its daily deliberations. If we speak of
love, light will answer, *Do you remember me?*

But beyond the light I look, now, parting the gray fabric
whose body and smell are simple things we may know
as we knew the soft last glaze of an eye,

as we know, in time, our own coarse fleshweight and the useless
discarded shape of a shoe, the world's garbage.
We are what the wind moves, scraps of litter
shunted against a fence somewhere, trying

to understand. Or if not that, simply to hold on and know
we are living, now, and nothing else matters. Yet we look
out of our rooms to see the green barn, burned
by wind, the fence diving over familiar hills,

a landscape of lime white in a sun cremating each particular.
We are of these particulars but we do not look
closely enough to know more than what
we have casually touched
until the wind slices
and whatever we leaned on is memory,

is the road I can see from her window, broiling and black,
where the last cars disappear at a mound of earth
under a pale, relaxed sky,

and is also the insatiable lust of the mind to stare down
into a yard where someone stirs a boiling pot
and hogs, snuffling for scraps, blindly
lunge body to body, great scrotums swinging,

their squeals of discovery and pleasure the same
scalded, in dissolution, cries we have made.

PINE CONES

Any way you hold them, they hurt.
What's the use, then?

Once in our backyard, by a sparrow's hidden
tremor there in the green wish of spruce,
a full but unfolded body

hung. It bore every color of the world and was sweet
beyond measure. The canyon wind banged
at this then went elsewhere.

Something happened that night.
The sparrow seems to have seen what it was.

Look at him huddled there, mistakably some other shadow,
the sly outlines of his body almost blue as spruce,
the sun like a big wall nearby

and you stepping through it, big, that big
he would almost give up his only wish.

Almost. Almost. Almost.

Isn't this the way hearts beat in the world,
the way pine cones fall in the night
until they don't?

When you pick them up, as children do,
the tiny spot appears in your palm,
red as the sun's first blink
of love.

And that sticking unabidable tar.

LOON

Kneeling,
you are without children.
The seeds of the pine
drop on the nightwind
and a cry comes your way,
in bent syllables,
over the small lake.
Looking out
from the dark porch
I try to find that
sound you turn to
as if it might swell
the breasts vacantly
you notice each night.

How difficult it is to know
the body that fits each
cry over stilled water,
to know that mouth
sinking under a tongue
of darkness when
something howls
in our dreams. If
we could hear that,
I think, if we could know
even the least gesture
of a seed buoyant
still in wet absence,
we might understand
grace and its song.

The loon, wire-white
as a star streaking,
triggered by reeds,
doesn't mean to grieve,
to cut this moment
with a child's shriek.
He is only trying
to say what he is,
swelling his space
with the news of
the debris he tastes.
Like you he doesn't know
what cry he hears but
goes on answering
in echoed praise
what he could not sing.

IN SNOW, A POSSIBLE LIFE

I am sitting there with my bitter self-taste,
Lael, Jeddie, Mary, and you asleep overhead
in the blue light I love, that snow-wash,
the glass doors locked and iced before me.
If I were not so cold I would go out
into that emptiness to find pure words.
Instead I think of the snow piling up, how
it is like sugar falling through a floor crack
at the foot of a dark mountain, some house
abandoned, the work done, the family gone.
Snow makes its slow statement and I think
of that house, its cold tools and sacked things.
In this way, without flash or any witness,
I have gone down there, a father trying to see
what to do in all this immense swirling. What
I have seen, all night, is the white surge
like a human hand lifted over the dirt
with its own form, its fate, to which
I am nothing watching. I should not stay here.
I should go where words make a clumsy shape
against this heavy drift, where the self
I am can speak its forgiveness in its own
house, in its own tongue. Lifting my eyes
I learn again the shape of your calm faces
and see the snow's light turn them luminous.
Whoever I am, whatever words I badly use,
may we come to the pure heat of our bodies
and keep in ourselves the dark edges
no snow in this world ever softened enough.

MORNING LIGHT: WANSHIP, UTAH

Trails of it like trout-streaks skid
the Weber River under the scald
of the interstate where swallows
roar past like trucks to build
what winter never remembers.

It has come suddenly, from the mountain,
to glow on the small girl whose hair
flies like feathers from the nest
of her gaze. She is dreaming
what moves inside that flow,

the line in her hand connecting her
to what laps at her hung foot. She
blinks at each dark zooming
of bird, as at a scar still pink
and unbelievable, and I hunch

in my shadow behind her, in slow burning
light that is pure fear, for I
know how greased with quick green
the rocks are, how cold spray
is like a handful of water dropped

from a lover's hand where a girl lies
sunning only for the first deep gaze
up into the dizzying sun, yes, and
the dead-face roll on the back
when memory can resolve nothing,

cannot even give back the face of a man
that somewhere, far upstream, waits.
What is joy but that first squint
of love through hardest light,
and the dreams roaring in futility?

Hours it seems I watch each split twig
fester toward a knot of steel-flaring
water where swallows swoop and take
what they need until at last
I lift my face and know I am

inside the dream no one ever wakes from.
In the terrible light of morning
each bird, each child is a dream
lodged until it slides out
of itself, becoming the vast pouring

dream the world is everywhere. It leans down
from the mountain to dapple the skin
of a small girl like a first peach.
Swallows scream in the air
for the grief of it, and the joy,

and I, seeing her turn upshoulder to look
into my face, want to warn her.
But what is there to say except
that she must remember this dream
brilliant as a dot of light

in a dark room? Far off on the mountainside
light spears twice and is only a man
on a battered tractor whose
dark face is unimaginable to me
but I squint as if I could see everything.

TO ANYONE HUNTING AGATES ON A
PACIFIC BEACH

Under cliffs as ragged as the world's first morning you are
the one who has shucked off the load of ideas that refused
to build a better world, the one who goes hours bent over
in outsized raingear, hair-feathering and bird-alert above
sand carved to a crumbling peninsula. Like a grim fugitive
from that exterior world of demands to the east, you tread
the edge of foam and unseen suck of current. I watch you
as if you were a dumb other self, feeling the cold seepage
in that forgotten slit of the boot. That and all else sifts
out through the now darting, now spread net of your hands.
The prospect of so much rubble is overwhelming. Anywhere,

you are thinking, there may be one more perfect than hope,
purple at its heart as a god's gown, blue as a mullet's eye.
It's this that bears you down, fragments that litter thick
in your pockets, a weight to drown you if the sand should
skid or you take a blind step. You won't look anywhere else
until the darkness begins to lock you in. Millions like you,
in any cheap mirror, would feel the emptiness of this place,
would straighten the kinked spine and walk away content with
legs sorely knotted. We know what they say: What good in it?
We agree, there is no cash in what's been heaved up from
the interior, nothing gold but the gold-slick of illusions.

The idea, then, is simple and takes you beyond that country
where the telephone is ringing with ancient obligations. I
have watched you enter this dream, if it is a dream, glittering
with the mind's assertive flow. It swirls around delight's
rock, plainly there, and the only need is this final searching.

I have seen this and want to tell you what is going to happen. The wind will, any moment, come screaming off the ocean where the last convulsion of sun glowers. Behind you a gaunt shadow hangs, crippled, ready to follow each step back along the iced thread of sand. The black suck of the surf will, now, hammer at your heart. Driving inland each house reminds you there was someone you loved but never enough, the odd way walls bow, the black sheen of empty streets. Understand, too, how so much follows from that first look up into the sun. It explains why you suddenly jump from your half-sleep where agates, like someone's eyes, gleam furiously at the darkness.

NIGHT, OUR HANDS PARTING THE BLUE AIR

It blooms in the chokeweed and breathes, turning
the air butternut and blue. A man
climbs the distant horizon, his steps
soundless in the leaves hung
almost reverently, but beginning
to tremble in tune with the first star.

He moves slowly and we are able to turn away while
the stalks of weed sing, while a light flows
from a kitchen window, then find him
as if nothing had changed, as if risen
darkness, like water, brought him
forth on the earth to make us forget ourselves.

Again and again we feel ourselves look away shyly
into the blue thickened behind us,
then back to that shape grown
half visible, and less. We feel
in such light there is no time to waste,

so begin the story that gathers the sweet breath
of our children. It says *Once upon a time* —
our voice dividing into groans
the wind made that night our father
left the road, our hands parting
the blue air branch after branch as we

wait in a room of light cast on the furred hillside.
Each sound of the cooling earth wants to become
our speech. We hear, we can hardly bear
not to leap up in joy and tears,
but there is only darkness and no one
sliding out of leaves where the world monstrously

gargles its syllables without meaning until we try,
driven red-eyed beyond sleep, to pray.
Calling the names of parents
who were the future and are,
now, the past, we want to fill
the dark with our hands, with ways
a man can get home. Somewhere
there is a path no one can get lost on

until the last hour of the world ends, each small head
lolling in a dream of the infinite undark.
We sink into ourselves as we invent
someone who loves us. He climbs the hill
where the gold has trickled deep blue.
Light from our kitchen falls into his eyes.
Night, giver of morning, comes on, swirling over us.

A GOLD OF BIRDS

Amidst some moment of grace, unrecognized though the world is
obvious for the most part, joy insinuates itself.
In Salt Lake City I have seen an unremarkable sun
drop behind Antelope Island like a bloodstain
on snow, until the world festered red

and all night, lying in a dark room, felt on each inch of skin
an unaccountable annoyance. The sheet lay on skin
acute, as with an extreme diabetic, until
I kicked it off and was naked
as a boy filling the room with his risen self,

but did not connect my jitters with either sunset or bloodshed
and hardly understand any juncture of eye and memory,
but know the grass everywhere had gone blood-bright
under a cloud-spattered blue sky and know

a swoop of small birds cut a gold scar in what I saw, that silence,
where the world seemed no more than itself. The island lay
ridged against the down-boiling light but was
far west and only shadow in any case,
yet I strained to hear any sound there might be,

and heard the whipping of those small wings, then saw the gold.
And saw one trailing bird shatter in the sudden scar
of the evening hawk that wheeled and was gone.
Saw the wreckage drop into the valley
whose trees reached up like black lake-stumps

and my body was rushing with excitement, for I was a young boy
walking home at dusk and my body smelled from the girl
I had loved, finally, and there just over the pine
he lifted at my coming, talons bloodied.

He did not flee, only circled to make that enormous screech
echoing over the river long gold in the last light.
I went on into shadows and stood to see him drop
onto the darkened horizon, but saw nothing
except in the nightlong dream and sweat of my joy

where a face, in gold frame of hair, floated, then fell from me.
Her face, years now slipped under the heavy sheet
where what I thought was pain gathered, but this
was only her dark secret, and is now

what I wake with, the whisper of joy kicking to be naked, gold,
silent as the first lips on your neck, gold
where what was blue goes red and bleeds itself empty.

Poetry from Illinois

History is Your Own Heartbeat
Michael S. Harper (1971)

The Foreclosure
Richard Emil Braun (1972)

The Scrawny Sonnets and Other Narratives
Robert Bagg (1973)

The Creation Frame
Phyllis Thompson (1973)

To All Appearances: Poems New and Selected
Josephine Miles (1974)

Nightmare Begins Responsibility
Michael S. Harper (1975)

The Black Hawk Songs
Michael Borich (1975)

The Wichita Poems
Michael Van Walleghen (1975)

Cumberland Station
Dave Smith (1977)

Tracking
Virginia R. Terris (1977)

Poems of the Two Worlds
Frederick Morgan (1977)

Images of Kin: New and Selected Poems
Michael S. Harper (1977)

On Earth As It Is
Dan Masterson (1978)

Riversongs
Michael Anania (1978)

Goshawk, Antelope
Dave Smith (1979)